The 5 Secret Buying Values

"Unlock the #1 Sales Technique on How to Sell More"

MATTHEW E ALLEYNE

This book is registered with The National Library of Norway.

ISBN-10: 8299889804
ISBN-13: 978-82-99889803

Cover Design & Layout by MyBrand Butler
www.MyBrandButler.com

The 5 Secret Buying Values™
www.The5SecretBuyingValues.com

DEDICATION

This book is dedicated to every salesperson who is struggling to thrive in a competitive marketplace. May you achieve closure again and again.

CONTENTS

ACKNOWLEDGMENTS

To Salespeople - You make the world go round. Logistics handles the deliver, accounting handles the finance, but a sale is what connects the customer to the perfect solution. Without salespeople, the world would be in utter chaos… because who ever really knows what they want in life? Thank you to every sales person for providing the path to the solution.

To Sales Leaders - Every team must have a leader that sets the example. For your morals, your ethics and your upstanding position in the market, I thank you for all that you do. You help to maintain the integrity of our industries, and never fail to remind the rest of us why we're here. To all that you have done in the past and present that we have learned from, I thank you.

To My Mother - For being a shining example in sales, and teaching me how to connect with people on a personal level, thank you for everything you've shown me. Rest in peace.

To Those I've worked with in the past - I've worked with countless sales people, but none have been forgotten. Were it not for the teams I've worked with in the past, this book would not exist. You revealed the doorway for so many others to benefits.

INTRODUCTION – FINDING VALUE IN VALUE

I've had an adventuresome heart since I was a small child, and a business savvy that began just as early. My first business was at the age of 9, where I ran a pick and pack service for a home party business my mother was running. While she sold the product, I worked at home to fill the orders.

For more than 25 years I've worked in sales, whether it was selling my own business or consulting with others to improve their own.

I've studied under, and worked with, some of the best known names in sales such as Zig Ziglar, Napoleon Hill, W Clement Stone and Brian Tracy. I now run a successful online marketing company, MyBrand Butler.

One of my most successful ventures was ROCKA, a multi-million dollar furniture franchise business that I established in Norway, the business started online. and then developed into retails stores. We enjoyed an 800% growth within the first 2 years.

In 2009, I was running a sales meeting with my staff to try to improve numbers. I couldn't understand why the staff just couldn't seem to sell like me. When I queried them, the response was simple.

"We can't all sell like you."

That created an "AHA" moment - why couldn't they sell like me? I began to dissect my own sales process and laid it out on paper. I knew I had to be more flexible with my sales team, so I set about finding the best way to make a sale - no matter who was selling. The 5 Secret Buying Values™ was born, and it was the perfect model because it was flexible enough to work for anyone on my team, and it was ideal for engaging the customer.

And in the end, that's what is important because the customer is the boss.

These are secret values, because customers don't even know they exist. These innate values become our secret weapon to connect with a customer and close the sale.

To my staff, it was like a light came on. They didn't replace their techniques, but incorporated it to improve their overall arsenal. And the results were amazing.

I saw some salespeople grow a little, while others doubled and tripled their sales figures.

I'm not reinventing the wheel, just showing you the most accurate way to close sales. No shortcuts, no tricks or gimmicks.

It's all about engagement and value.

And it's guaranteed to work!

Selling is one of the highest paid jobs in the world, with top level performers in the industry hunted for their skill, prowess and ability to close.

Without sales, companies close. Without an understanding of value, the sales process becomes hit or miss, with a heavy lean toward missing. In order to survive, you must learn not just how to sell effectively, but how to lead the customer into making a buying decision.

Selling isn't enough; the customer has to buy into you. Making a connection through The 5 Secret Buying Values™ establishes a relationship with customers that can turn any sales person into a millionaire.

There are more millionaires in this industry than anywhere else, and it's not because they have 30 or more years' experience. It's because they understand how to connect with the customer. They know how to make every sale a win-win.

I'm not here to explain the mechanics of making the perfect sale.

You're not here to learn the basics. You're here to understand the most effective techniques to supplement an already killer strategy.

Now you can join the ranks of all the other salespeople before you that have made the sales industry what it is today.

Sales has its ups and downs, and you won't always be riding on the ups - but with what I'm about to show you, you'll be able to do more than just survive.

To Your Sales Success,

Matthew E Alleyne

1 WHAT ARE VALUES?

A value is simple; it is a belief, a mission or a philosophy that has meaning to an individual. In some cases we are consciously aware of values, in some cases we are not. Regardless of our self-awareness, we all have a core set of personal values that define our daily thoughts, decisions, reactions, choices, etc.

Those values can range from the more common beliefs, such as hard work or punctuality, to the more psychological and in-depth stuff such as self-reliance, harmony of purpose, and compassion or concern for others.

If we take the time to examine the lives of well-known people, we can often see how decisions were made - chained together by personal values. Those values greatly influenced the decisions that propelled them to the top of their fields.

Whatever the personal values of the individual, we very often take them to heart, where they manipulate, influence and control even the smallest details of our lives.

Like a purchase.

Just as individuals inherently subscribe to various values, so to do organizations and commercial business have a set of values. If you were to dissect any company, you would discover that one or more of those companies had values at the core of their success.

Sears has a commitment to trusting the customer, evident by the fact that any product could be returned to the company with a money back guarantee. It created trust in both directions with customers, it created a sales boom for the company and Sears experienced a wealth of growth as a result.

Apple held to its values in solving problems for society. A fine example in their values is the creation and marketing of the iPod and iTunes store, effectively bridging the gap between consumers who wanted to download music and obtain it at reduced rates and the music industry which pushed back against digital downloads.

Marriott valued systemization and standardization. By creating a standard hotel model, the company was able to duplicate it hundreds of times around the globe. This created rapid growth opportunities and transformed Marriott into one of the leaders in the hospitality industry.

Businesses operate with values because they are driven by people. Whether it's a political organization, a commercial business, a club, a fellowship or a non-profit, there are core human values at work.

Without values we would be mechanical, driven to action and reaction by unpleasant situations in life. It would be a feral existence, with people taking action based solely on urges and passion.

When it comes to sales and closing deals, we certainly want people to be driven by passion. To settle on urges and impulse.

But we need those values to help us, as a sales force, to define what is right for our audience, and how we can connect with them to best serve those interests.

We cannot see them, or touch them, but values are every bit as real as any physical object. There are people who devote their entire lives to understanding and pursuing certain values (such as those loyal patriots who gave their lives fighting for the values of freedom and equality). Values are psychological objects.

My goal is to help you identify the most important values to a customer, because those values influence every buying decision they make. What you think matters toward making a sale, and what matters to the customer (both consciously and subconsciously), are very different.

The next page is a table with just a few examples of the various types of values people may focus on - values that drive their everyday decisions.

Common Personal Values That Influence Daily Decisions

Accomplishment, Success
Accountability
Accuracy
Adventure
All for one & one for all
Beauty
Calm, quietude, peace
Challenge
Change
Charity
Cleanliness, orderliness
Collaboration
Commitment
Communication
Community
Competence
Competition
Concern for others
Connection
Content over form
Continuous improvement
Cooperation
Coordination
Creativity
Customer satisfaction
Decisiveness
Determination
Delight of being, joy
Democracy
Discipline
Discovery
Diversity
Dynamism
Ease of Use
Efficiency
Enjoyment
Equality
Excellence
Fairness
Faith
Faithfulness
Family
Family feeling
Flair
Gentleness
Global view
Goodwill
Goodness
Gratitude
Hard work
Happiness
Harmony
Health
Independence
Individuality
Inner peace, calm, quietude
Innovation
Integrity
Intelligence
Intensity
Justice
Kindness
Knowledge
Leadership
Love, Romance
Loyalty
Maximum utilization
(of time, resources)

Meaning
Merit
Money
Oneness
Openness
Other's point of view, inputs
Patriotism
Peace, Non-violence
Perfection
Personal Growth
Perseverance
Pleasure
Power
Practicality
Preservation
Privacy
Progress
Reliability
Resourcefulness
Respect for others
Responsiveness
Results-oriented
Rule of Law
Safety
Satisfying others
Security
Self-givingness
Self-reliance
Self-thinking

Sensitivity
Service
(to others, society)
Simplicity
Skill
Solving Problems
Speed
Spirit, Spirituality in life
Stability
Standardization
Status
Strength
Succeed; A will to-
Success, Achievement
Systemization
Teamwork
Timeliness
Tolerance
Tradition
Tranquility
Trust
Truth
Honor
Human-centered
Improvement
Unity
Variety
Well-being
Wisdom

2 WHY WE BUY

The Fundamentals of Purchasing

If you break down the purchase of a particular item, there's a lot going on in the formulate that brought a person to close. Not only are there emotional factors but you also have to consider branding and marketing, needs, wants, desires, values - the list goes on. While values are only a portion of what closed a deal, they have a lot of weight to throw around when you start stacking them up against emotion.

The fundamentals of sales circle around the concept that if you understand the triggers that make people buy then you can sell them more. A common mistake in sales however is that some think that people feel compelled to buy only by emotional need, or to fill a solution, or because they just purchase what they need.

The fact is, people buy what they want to buy when a given product resonates with specific values.

It's rarely needs. Think about the most popular items going on the market today and start ticking off the people in your life you know who absolutely need the following items:

- 46" HDTV with 1080p 60hz refresh
- iPod Nano
- Kindle Fire
- Playstation3/Xbox360
- $200 Basketball Shoes

Sales reps often mistake their market for people who need the product. If you focus on convincing people who need your product to want it, you'll never succeed. The best target market for any sales rep is the people who want the product.

What you need to do is appeal to their core values and make them realize - consciously - that they want this product. When you can install a sense of want, then they will generate the need for it.

Break it down to something simple like food: We all need to eat, but no one needs to sit down with a sirloin steak smothered in grilled shrimp. We don't need a Black Forest premium cut ham and provolone deli sub, and we don't need a deep dish pizza. We eat those things because we want them.

The needs of your customer are something very logical, and very matter of fact. As people we have physical and emotional needs. How we satisfy each of our individual needs are largely directed by urgency, our values and our perception of the need based on our wants.

Those wants for the items we buy - often on impulse, are directed by core values and emotions. When you combine core values with the strongest emotions that exist in every person you can begin to make stronger connections with customers.

Value and Emotional Triggers

Understanding the value and emotion reasons why customers buy from you, from brands, specific products, for people, etc. then you can unlock how to pull these triggers with your prospects and customers.

Love

What is it that your customers are in love with? Is it an idea? A person? A place? We all know that love, or the feelings that surround it, can drive people to do strange and wonderful things. From businesses and careers to culture, hobbies and pets, love can be a powerful influencer.

Pride

If pride is something of a sin, then we're all guilty. We swell with pride over the smallest things. I'm personally proud of my achievement as a best-selling author. I am proud of my friends who have achieved so much in life despite barriers. I'm proud of my own accomplishments that led me to acquire certain "toys". I am proud to be a Kiwi at heart from New Zealand.

Think about how you felt when you bought that first new car and pulled into your driveway? It was a swell of pride, and you likely hoped that others were watching.

Guilt

If you don't think guilt is a common factor in line with buying values, then think again. The real reason purchases are made - or allowed to be made - can originate with guilt. One of the core values for a customer may be the strength of the family unit, and out of guilt over a fight with his wife that customer may feel compelled to not only send flowers but to spend more than $800 on a new dress, dinner, shoes and an expensive cruise around the city harbor.

That train of thought can lead you to wonder how many gifts originate from guilt, even those on Christmas, Valentines, Mothers' Day, etc.

Can the guilt of not purchasing something spur you into a purchase? What about the guilt that children use to manipulate their parents into a purchase?

Fear

Fear can be a powerful driving force when it comes to sales. This emotion, entwined with core values, has likely had a large role in helping humanity survive. We have grown and learned to fear many things, and those fears can be effectively used to help customers and prospects associate wants with needs.

Many customers and prospects don't necessarily think about which decision is the right one. It's that they fear making the wrong decision and the consequences that come with it.

How can you use the association of values and their other emotions to diminish or eliminate those fears?

Greed

When you boil it down, Gordon Gecko from the movie Wall Street nailed it. "Greed is Good". If you're in sales then that concept shouldn't shock you. You need to sell to the greedy, not to the needy. The people who are greedy focus on their wants and they're willing to pay for it.

The needy may be needy not out of a lack of funding, but because they don't really want it bad enough.

It's easier to take a greedy person and use their values and emotions to transform a want into a need, than to take an average Joe and transform their need into a want.

3 HOW BUYING VALUES INFLUENCE SALES

Great Sales Require More than Greatness

In 2001, Jim Collins wrote the best-selling book, *Good to Great*, that turned the attentions of business people around the world toward "Greatness". Why is it that some companies do so well when a similar competitor starts to falter and weaken in the industry? Why is it that some companies launch to greatness quickly? What traits and behaviors separate the good companies and salespeople from the great ones?

The concept we hear regularly in sales circuits is that if you're going to go to work, you might as well go all the way. Shoot for the pinnacle of success, be competitive, set your sights high and push. If you're going to invest the time and the risk in selling, then strive for greatness.

The problem is that this focus on greatness is great as a motivational exercise, but it does very little to close deals and sell customers. Customers don't care if you're having a good day, if you feel great, if you're persistent in your success.

Striving to be great doesn't sell, and pushing too hard in that direction can be a wasted effort.

Don't misunderstand - I believe in self-motivation. Whatever you do to get out of bed in the morning and give it your all is important. The problem is when people start focusing too much on what makes a company or a salesperson great. When that happens, they forget how to sell.

Focusing on Traits over Values

There are a lot of traits out there that people in sales and marketing believe you must have in order to sell a customer and get to a close.

That includes:

- **Character** - Being ethical and honest
- **Competitive spirit** - Motivating yourself to win
- **Interpersonal skills** - Possessing a certain level of charisma
- **Strategic thinking** - Planning around the bigger picture
- **Focus** - Understanding your competencies and refining them
- **Functioning Under Stress** - Keeping a level head in any sales situation

Truthfully, these are all important. But they are also nothing more than common sense traits when it comes down to doing good business. They provide a good foundation for forming a relationship with a customer but a foundation is not a home. In order to close sales and move a customer toward a purchase you need to find what appeals to them.

You need to understand their ***values****.*

In chapter 2 we discussed generic values that everyone has, and there are a lot of them. Those play some measurable role in a sale, but in an indirect way. There are 5 core values that determine how and why people buy a product or a service, and the majority of our generic values tie into one or more of those 5 values in some specific way.

Before we get into that, let's take a look at The 5 Secret Buying Values™ in more detail.

The 5 Secret Buying Values™

Design

Design has a great deal of influence on whether or not someone purchases a product or hires a company for a service. People are visual by nature, that's why marketing uses colors to garner specific reactions. There are a variety of tried and tested designs that are guaranteed to bring out certain kinds of results. Most customers include design in their purchase decision, but it's not limited to the product itself. Judging and choosing to buy by design can factor in a lot of aesthetic and visual variables.

- **Product design**
- Packaging style & color
- **Uniforms of employees & sales staff**
- Design and layout of a store or sales floor
- **Office decor**
- Landscaping
- **General cleanliness**

Design always has a strong influence because the right design can appeal to the inner nature and primitive, subconscious preferences.

Neuromarketing is the buzz right now, and design plays a big part in neuromarketing, specifically in how products are designed to appeal to a customer. A classic example? The Mini-Cooper. Research into Neuromarketing and how the brain works revealed that the same parts of the brain that light up when you see the new Mini are the same parts the light up with electrical and chemical reactions when you see a baby. Really. A baby. There's just something about the shape that makes people think "small infant" when they see the car - and that attractive design is what helps close the sale.

Quality

You would think that a lot of people put a great deal of focus on quality, but it's more important to some people than others. For a penny-pincher, they know they can save money and they we're willing to take a hit on quality if it means knocking a percentage off the final bill.

For those who do focus on quality, they typically believe that a brand name is more important than price and they associate popular brands with higher quality. Where quality is concerned as a primary value, a customer will often demand that a salesperson be extremely knowledgeable about the products and services. When a customer is judging quality, they're not necessarily wondering whether the product will last for years, they want to know that the product is safe, is made with the latest technology (as opposed to inferior outdated technology) and - where consumables are concerned - they tend to focus on ingredients and the nutritional content.

An important point to note is that where quality is concerned, a customer is often far less concerned about price. There is a stigma that in order to get quality, you must pay for it.

Availability

In 2010, Nordstrom gave its online shoppers access to local store inventory, and customers are responding. According to Jamie Nordstrom, president of Nordstrom Direct, they made the change "because the No.1 call we got at our call center was, 'Hey, I'm looking at this item online, can I look at it at my store?'

Sharing local product availability was credited as a primary reason that Nordstrom has seen a same-store increase of 8% since the implementation. The primary goal was to get their multi-channel shoppers into the store since they "spend four times, on average, what a one-source shopper does."

The change not only increased in-store visits and purchases, it also improved inventory turnover and cost margins. Now, when online stock is depleted, customers can locate the product in any of Nordstrom's 115 stores. "By pulling merchandise from the store, you've dramatically lessened the likelihood that you'll take a markdown," noted Nordstrom in an article in the New York Times.

There's two ways to look at availability and how it can influence sales. It all boils down to supply and demand. By having certain product and services where there is a demand for them, particularly when there are competitors that do not offer it or have it, you can benefit from the demand.

Communicating the limited availability, while you have a dominant control of the stock and a "can't get it anywhere else" situation, you can improve the odds of an immediate close on a sale.

This also allows you to leverage urgency. When customers know an offer, product or service is limited they are far more likely to buy.

From the example above, we see the other side of availability. Always keeping products and services available in the most convenient manner can turn a customer on to closing a sale when they recognize the quality of the service and the great length a company goes to in order to keep products available at all times.

Availability does not work for everyone, because there are some customers who are not influenced by supply and demand. That's why it's important to understand where availability falls in the value chain of a customer.

Price

As mentioned above in the section on quality, price can be important for some but it isn't always factor for everyone. There are those who won't pull out their wallet even for the best sale (because they don't connect their values to how the product is being marketing) and there are those who will pay whatever they need to pay to get a product or service (because they understand the value - a connection was made)

Too many salespeople approach price from the wrong angle, focusing on value proposition and the actual price over the cost benefit of the customer. Here's a great example of an improper focus and how it can hurt a business.

Mary, a dance instructor, learned the difference between value proposition and cost benefit when one of her students didn't return for the new fall season. The student, Lisa, had been studying for two years and was ready to move to a more advanced level. When Mary spoke with Lisa's mother and relayed the exciting news, she changed the schedule that put Lisa in the advanced class. Shortly thereafter, Jenny dropped out.

Advancement meant more classes, more time and in turn more money from the student. Mary assumed that progression to the next level was natural and a given requirement. The family didn't agree because the cost benefit was too low, and advancement was not presented as optional.

Lisa's cost benefit outweighed Mary's value proposition.

Eventually, Mary called and apologized for making the assumption.

Lisa's mom was happy to know they were welcome to return at a recreational level, but not this year because Jenny had already committed to another activity.

Mary's professional dance career caused her to create a value proposition from a narrower lens than the wide angle lens of her market. Most of the students at the dance school don't have professional aspirations. Parents see it as a recreational activity, or a social one that offers other opportunities, role models, etc. Few are ready to make professional commitments.

Mary has now evolved her value proposition to leverage this wide array of customer cost benefits. She recognizes that each student and parent has a unique set of desires and needs. She and the instructors learn what each student and family expects from the program – their cost benefit.

So when price is a factor, and becomes dominant in the buying values chain, forget your value proposition. Even if you have a great deal of research behind you, your value proposition is still generalized.

It helps you connect with the customer in order to establish your value chain (more on the value chain in the next section) but it won't always help you close. At the end of the day, a customer focused on price buys based on their unique cost benefit.

Never assume to know your customer's cost benefit.

Your customers expect unique outcomes, some of which are hidden in a back room few salespeople ever enter. To sit on the customer's side of the table you must convince them that their needs and desires are your priority. Crafting questions and listening with your eyes, ears, neurons, hormones, and instincts is the key to the private room where customers make decisions.

Functionality

Functionality is an area where salespeople commonly fall short on making a sale. While functionality is important where a product or service is concerned, the most important thing to remember is that a customer doesn't care about your product. What you sell means absolutely nothing to them.

Don't Sell the Steak - Sell the Sizzle

They don't care if it's a blue or black widget. They don't care if it's large or small. You can start talking features and functionality until you're blue in the face but it won't make a sale. Even if someone is looking for that product, they might not know it's the right product by listing off the functionality.

What sells people is the connection between their problem or their need and the functionality and features of a product.

When you provide an obvious solution to their greatest pain point then you're one step closer to sealing the deal.

The key is understanding the benefits that are associated with the features, and the solutions those features provide. When you're getting a feel for the value chain of your customer, and you're listening to their problem, or their need, you'll be able to quickly connect which of the features and benefits are most likely to appeal to them. That connection lights up a path to a solution like a well-lit airport runway.

Tell your customers, very specifically, what's in it for them.

The Feature/Benefit Matrix

Functionality only goes so far. Here are some prime examples of how you can transform features and functionality into benefits.

Functionality/Features	**Benefits**
Our firm only employs attorneys with at least 15 years' experience	• No fear of inexperienced, new attorneys • Entire team is familiar with a broad range of legal issues • All types of law dealt with - one-stop source • Leading experts in individual legal divisions

Our agency employs 8 professional writers	• Each writer targets a different niche, and can write any form of content for that niche • Large team of writers means rapid turnaround without loss of quality • Work with multiple writers and choose the best one that fits your company
Our warehouse is over 150,000 sq. ft.	• Every product in stock • Never a backorder issue • Same day shipping • Carry more parts than other competitors, and most parts that stores don't carry
Free Shipping	• Reduce overall spend on products • Turn shipping costs into an extra item or an upgrade • Get the latest technology /goods at reduced cost over competitors

These are just examples, but it shows that every industry - whether you're selling a product or a service - has features that you commonly use to sell. What you need to do in order to connect with the functionality values with a customer is to reveal the benefits of those features and answer the fundamental question:

"What's in it for me?" WIIFM

A quick exercise: Think about the product you sell the most often, and the features you highlight when promoting or selling it. Act out offering that product to someone using the features, then ask yourself "So?". Force yourself to elaborate. After you elaborate on the feature, ask again. "So?". And elaborate further. This exercise in "What's in it for me" helps you drill down the features to create a very targeted list of benefits.

How Your General Values Ties Into the 5 Buying Values

We see how each of these values is important, but how do all those general values we spoke about earlier tie into just those 5 core buying values?

Every person is different, and they all have different values that drive them. A great example is Patriotism from our big table of values in Chapter 2. If you speak with a customer and discover their patriotic streak is strong, that can tell you a lot about their core values.

A US customer that is patriotic likely:

- Proudly buys American products
- May be concerned about design, particularly where a design might have a patriotic position. (i.e. Made in America, Imported from Detroit, etc.)
- Believes that American made is important, and that American products are higher quality
- May have a very high focus on quality in the product
- May have reduced concern for cost, because they know they will spend more buying American made quality products

Just knowing that the customer is patriotic isn't enough to establish a complete value chain, but depending on their focus on that value it may help you determine whether or not something like Quality is at the peak of their value chain.

One more example from the table of values in the last chapter would be Decisiveness. A customer who is calculating and decisive is likely to be far more analytical than a customer who buys on a whim. Someone who is able to reason out a purchase quickly, with strong analytic skills, is likely to focus more on values like availability - do they really need it right now or is it something I can just come back for later? They may also focus on function and the real benefit. They would likely combine the need with the want to determine if it's a smart purchase.

Getting the Value Chain Right

I speak a lot about the value chain, because this is where the 5 core buying values come together. Every customer you work with makes a buying decision based on the 5 core secret buying values, and their overall, general values and emotions play a part in shaping the order of importance of those values.

That means there's a lot of variation in how people, even with those 5 core values.

Let's take a look at these 3 customers and examine how two approaches to buying a television would change based on how their values are prioritized in their mind, with value #1 being the most important.

Customer 1	**Customer 2**	**Customer 3**
1. Price	1. Availability	1. Quality
2. Functionality	2. Price	2. Functionality
3. Design	3. Design	3. Design
4. Availability	4. Quality	4. Availability
5. Quality	5. Functionality	5. Price

The first customer is price shopping for a television. He likely wants to get the best features for his money. He would love to get a 1080p LCD flat screen with a high refresh rate but he sees that the big brands are really expensive. He'll have to sacrifice some of the features he wants to save, but what he doesn't like about cheaper models is the size.

Where design is concerned he also wants a larger model. He's not too concerned about the sales right now, even though some of them might be ending soon, because he'll likely buy something today. If he doesn't, it's no sweat. He's just not that influenced by availability. He's also not too concerned about quality. He's willing to buy a really cheap brand as long as he can get the features he wants.

Compare that to Customer #3

The last customer wants the highest quality television he can find. He's been walking back and forth along the wall of flat screen televisions at Best Buy for an hour and a half comparing picture quality and functionality of all the different brands.

He has some focus on design as far as size, but his biggest concern is getting a television that won't ghost when the frame rate of a video game goes up - or during an action intense sports game. Availability and price is at the bottom of his list.

You can see how the value chain can vary widely with your customers. This is where salespeople make a grave error - they try to impose their own value chain on the customer when trying to sell the product. The result is an over-emphasis on something that doesn't matter to the customer.

Imagine if you approached customer #3 and assumed that his indecisive wandering around the televisions meant he was price shopping and just couldn't choose the right television. If you tried to offer up some of the nice models at a discount price, you would immediately create a wedge between the two of you and he would see you as an interruption to his analytical process of choosing a TV - essentially you're bothering him, because he's not shopping by price.

If your buying value chain, and the buying value chain of your customer, is widely out of sync then the odds of closing the sale plummet and you can actually drive a customer away - even if they're ready to buy right now.

The key to making that connection when selling to a customer is to alter your own value chain to match that of the person you're selling to. To discern what is most important to them. You query their interests, needs, pain points, wants, etc. and slowly establish which is a priority.

4 HOW TO ESTABLISH CUSTOMER VALUES

What Does "Active Listening" Really Mean?

There's no shortage of bloggers out there shilling advice to sales people who will tell you to listen to the customer and build your business accordingly. The problem is, a lot of them have taken the concept too far.

I had an experience with a company in the past that had the wrong approach to marketing a product we had created. They finished their presentation and I was wrapping things up with standard questions.

Me: What's on your roadmap for us?

Technical Officer: We're going to listen to what you need.

The concept is sound, but notice how it also evades the important question - almost like a politician. The technical officer might as well have told me "The future is whatever you make it, and it's whatever you think it should be." He may have been trying to demonstrate that he was receptive, but it's a non-answer.

With further follow-up questions, I never got the answer I was looking for. Perhaps because they don't have enough customers to know where to actually take our product.

Additional questions looked like this:

> *Me: Do you have any questions for us?*
>
> *Technical officer: Yes. What is your biggest business problem that you would like someone to solve?*

I felt like they were fishing for ideas and asking me to define their next product for them. This is the kind of mistake a lot of businesses are making now. This isn't listening. This is rudderless ship.

Having clear goals and confidence is compatible with customer-guided development. What you should be doing is active listening. When you're speaking to customers and a suggestion manifests itself, make note of it. Restate it in your own words as you speak to the customer to make sure that you accurately understand their needs and concerns.

That is active listening, and it shows the customer that you understand where they're coming from.

Even if you're dealing with a customer who is buying a one-off product, and you're never likely to seek them again, there is still a need for relationship building. That requires back and forth communication. As you speak, you can begin to understand their problems. From there, it's a matter of prioritizing them.

In all cases you'll see that you're simultaneously engaging the customer and honing their values so you can create your value chain. That engagement means the customer will feel like you're genuinely listening and giving thoughtful consideration.

Because you are!

Honing and prioritizing their needs and values gives you the subject matter to focus on, and helps you establish your plan of attack on how to begin making the sale once you've established that basic relationship.

Steve Jobs Didn't Listen to Customers

It was obvious during the launch of the iPad that Steve Jobs didn't listen (or didn't put much emphasis on) customer research. To quote him: "We do no market research. We don't hire consultants".

And yet – or should that be because of – this refusal to pay much attention to what customers say they want, Apple has become the ultimate game changer.

If history repeats itself we will be asking ourselves in two years, "How did we ever do without the iPad?". Jobs' determination to carve his company's own path to innovation is an example of why you need to be bold to win in business today.

And that includes how you listen to customers.

Or indeed whether.

Henry Ford supposedly said if he had asked his customers what they wanted, before coming up with the Model T, they'd have asked for a faster horse. Tom Peters and others have long pointed out that the customers least likely to help you move on to the next innovation are the biggest customers you have. For B2B suppliers, those customers who provide most of your profit today are those whose views you pay most attention to. Yet ask them what they want and it is likely to be the usual thing – better, faster, cheaper. They want a better version of what they've already got.

Jobs was adept at seeing beneath the surface, at tuning into what customers wanted - they just didn't actively realize it until it was presented to them. This ability is best expressed by the German word 'Zeitgeist' - The emerging spirit of the age or mood of the moment. For you, it best translates to customer or market readiness.

People like Jobs succeeded because they listened differently, and paid attention to what people were ready for, even before they knew they were ready for it.

When you understand and utilize the 5 secret buying values as part of your sales process, you're able to tune into what people really want. They may not openly admit, in a vocal manner, that their biggest concern is quality, or price, but in listening appropriately you can determine that. Once you start to match your sales techniques to their value chain, the customer will feel like you know exactly what they need. It just makes sense.

Not because they know they shop by quality, or by price, or design, but because the way you propose it feels so damn right.

Look for the unspoken needs, not just what existing customers are already asking for, or what existing competitors are doing. That direction only leads to competitive convergence. A big pile of "sameness".

Also known as mediocrity. And mediocrity doesn't sell.

Changing Your Marketing Message Based on Gender

Some believe that when you're actively listening to customers, you have to watch for cues that are gender specific and keep certain stereotypes in mind. Committing to selling by gender stereotypes increases the likelihood of alienating a customer before you've had the opportunity to connect with them.

When you approach customers, wipe any gender association from your mind. Approaching them as an individual in search of a solution. This puts the focus on listening and establishing their value chain.

No two people are exactly identical down to every interest, general value and psychological development. We all reason differently, we have different logic responses. We make choices based on different factors and we buy for different reasons. None of which are based solely on gender.

Women are certainly more likely than men to buy cosmetic products, but their reason behind why they buy it, which brands they choose, the colors, etc. are based on needs and values that differ from person to person.

When you're selling a product, no part of your approach - listening included - should focus on gender. If you specifically work to actively listen and develop the value chain, you'll establish the most appropriate approach for that person - be they man or woman.

5 GET THE CUSTOMER TO BUY INTO THEIR VALUES

In sales, the ultimate goal is to pull a "yes" from a customer. This is what psychologists call "compliance". We're exposed to compliance in our youth, where we strive to get a "yes" from parents. We grow up seeking compliance for things in life, with much of what we do based in "yes" and "no" zones.

My first real exposure to the idea of compliance wasn't in school in a psychology book though. It was in the backyard with my Uncle, many years ago. As our elders often do, he wanted to show me something he knew I would enjoy. So he showed me something amazing with a stick that had a bunch of red feathers taped to it.

In a tree in his backyard there was a large nest where a family of robins was nesting. We worked our way over to the tree and he told me to raise the feather end of stick slowly up to the nest.

When the male robin saw the feathers, it immediately attacked them and started flapping its wings angrily as it chirped over and over. I laughed, but was confused and dumbfounded.

My uncle explained to me that the red feathers made the robin territorial. He wasn't able to explain why but he reasoned that the color was likely similar to another robin and the bird felt it was invading the nest. It is their instinct to attack other robins on sight when territory is an issue.

The Magic of Fixed Action Patterns

I've seen other experiments since then that were similar, where a robin would attack red feathers, but not an exact replica of a robin that was missing red feathers. This is an example of what scientists call "fixed-action patterns" in animals. A fixed action pattern is a precise and predictable sequence of behavior. It's instinctive, an automatic response. This sequence is set in motion by a specific "trigger."

Fixed-action patterns are common among animals. But what about humans? What if you could use a trigger to set off a desirable sequence of behavior in a potential customer — like saying "yes" to a request you make?

It's possible, and not only can you get a "yes" once, but you can get it five times to match with each of the core buying values of a customer.

In *Influence: The Psychology of Persuasion*, Robert B. Cialdini, a respected social scientist and specialist in the area of compliance psychology, says that "… automatic, stereotyped behavior is prevalent in much of human action …"

In the book, Cialdini points to an experiment by Harvard social psychologist Ellen Langer, where you witness this concept in action. Langer approached people waiting in line to use a copy machine and asked, "Excuse me, I have five pages. May I use the Xerox machine?" About 60% said "yes."

Under similar circumstances, she did the same thing, but instead asked, "Excuse me, I have five pages. May I use the Xerox machine because I have to make some copies?" In this case, an overwhelming 93% said "yes."

What happened to increase the "yes" response so dramatically?

People respond more openly to an idea or a concept when there is a reason. A reason helps people come to a decision, whereby they justify their actions. What's interesting about this experiment is that "because I have to make some copies" doesn't provide additional information - it's not a reason.

It is successful however due to the use of "because" which has grown to be a trigger. Once the trigger is learned, it's powerful enough to set in motion a behavior sequence. In this case, a "yes" response even in the absence of a concrete rationale.

Powerful Compliance Triggers for the Value Chain

When you're selling, it's easy to see the importance of fixed action patterns in how people buy. All you really need to know is, with your particular customers, what is their "stick and red feathers" that creates a yes response.

Reciprocation - People tend to have an overwhelming urge to repay debts, or to do something in return when something is done for them. This natural, deep-seated urge is so strong, noted paleontologist Richard Leaky has said that it is the very essence of what it means to be human. Sociologist Alvin Gouldner points out that no society on Earth escapes the reciprocity principle.

How do you apply it? Give something to a customer in relation to the value you're targeting. Whoever is receiving the gift will naturally feel like they're indebted to you. It doesn't have to be innately valuable, what's important is that it's perceived to be valuable. That means it can be a free book, planning kit, samples, subscriptions, service plans, special reports, or even time. Anything related to your product or service can be leveraged, as long as it's given freely. That urge to repay can often seat someone to say yes.

Commitment and Consistency - When it comes to the value chain, this is extremely important. You're not just getting someone to say yes once, but five times. People are naturally driven to remain consistent in our attitudes, words and actions. When we're led to make commitments, or go on record, or make a decision, then there is an urge to remain consistent to our original commitment.

The key to closing a sale is to get that initial commitment. It may appear small and innocent, because they're committing to a yes on a single value in the buying process - just one small idea. This commitment leads to a greater compliance as you begin to sell them on the rest of the value chain, and ask for a larger commitment to close the sale.

To apply it - ask for that small yes on the first trigger and begin to build on it. Salespeople refer to this as the "foot-in--the-door" technique. This sets up the psychological commitment. There's no money changing hands, no signatures going on record, but you're getting that mental commitment that is difficult to break. No matter how small, you'll be able to build on it.

Social Proof - Unless you live on a mountain and don't interact with others, you've likely turned to other people for guidance. If you're reading this book and you're involved in sales, then you're here because you're uncertain about something and want a little direction.

We frequently do this with the people we know.

We want to know what others think, how they feel, their overall opinion, how they react, etc. Once we learn from them, we act accordingly and are more comfortable about making decisions - because we feel protected by the power of social proof.

How to leverage social proof? When you're working through the value chain, show your customer how others use the service or buy the products. Relate stories and testimonials of other customers with a similar value chain. You can also flash pictures of customers with your products or using your services. Case studies are also fantastic social proof. When people see that others in a similar position as them that they can relate to (a similar value chain) they are more likely to move forward on their own.

Likability - It doesn't matter how well you sell someone on their 5 values, you can't force people to like you. It's a simple truth that people like to do business with people they like, and as a customer you know you're far more likely to say "yes" to someone, repeatedly, when you like them.

We readily comply with requests from those who are similar to us and for whom we have good feelings. It's what makes refusing to buy Tupperware from a friend or relative next to impossible.

Applying it is simple: Be personal and likable. This is one element of selling that most people know instinctively, but often fail to put into action. You might think it's easy to get people to like you, and you might think that a smile and personality is all it takes, but your customer knows that your purpose is the sell them something.

Where you have to succeed is in showing them you're there to give first and receive last - give them value and education, but above all else be real. Reveal who you are and show feelings. Tell stories they can relate to. Don't falsely flatter and praise, but present your message in a way that is appealing to their personal interests and likes. That can make you more likable, and help you build a stronger relationship with your customer. You become an ally for helping them solve their problems, address concerns and reach their goals.

Authority - We may be a world of independent spirits but we're still prone to response to authority. We turn to experts or those we perceive as experts, to give us answers and show us the path toward a solution. It is far easier to follow the path of an expert, as opposed to finding our own way through trial and error.

Even symbols of authority, like titles and clothing, can be enough to trigger a yes response on the value chain.

Example: Note how seeing someone with a white smock and stethoscope instantly suggests "doctor" and makes anything that person says about medicine seem more authoritative.

To apply it to your sales process in working through the value chain, provide some kind of sign or symbol of expertise. The most basic application is provide solid information on the product or service. This includes understanding how it applies to the problems the customer has and how they can benefit from it. This points back to early sections that detail the importance of showing customers the benefits of your product or service.

You can also cite or show credentials, awards, reviews and other similar marks of authority to improve trustworthiness and credibility.

Scarcity - Scarcity focuses on the buying value of availability. In general, the fear of loss is more powerful than the hope of gain. By properly engaging the instinctive tendency to avoid losing something - or avoid losing the chance to possess something desirable - you can trigger a "yes" response with scarcity.

First Contact - Identify the Customer Value Chain

Above all else, remember this; The fastest way to find the customers value chain is to start by asking them to disclose it! Do this through two simple steps. Start talking with your customer and

1. Introduce and sell the product with your own buying value for that specific product. This anchors you and sets the stage for building a relationship because the customer sees that you're not trying to sell them - you're sharing your own personal value and interests. It leads the customer into revealing what they really want.

This also sets you up for the most important question that will help you identify their #1 value…

2. Once the intro is complete, ask them the right question - the one that is the tell-all. It will reveal the deepest buying secret that is most important to them.

"Is that what's important to you?"

In almost every situation, the customer will be inclined to reply with what they believe to be their most important buying value. This begins the relationship building because they see the item from your perspective and you understand theirs. From here you engage the customer, talk about their other needs and build out the remaining 4 values using the techniques above.

It's important to note that all of these do not work all of the time with all of your customers. That's where listening comes into play. As you engage with your customer and establish a relationship, you'll put together a customer strategy that leads them to a "yes" in each buying value.

Remember, the 5 secret buying values are valid with ***every*** customer. It's not a matter of whether they have 3 out of 5 values relevant to their purchase. They associate with all 5. It's just a matter of discovering how they prioritize those values so you know which ones to emphasize.

Once you tier together their buying values in the right order, you can systematically put a small "yes" in place for each one. Once you have a small commitment, as I outlined previously, you can move forward with the big close by repeating their buying values back to them. Not only will that final "yes" be easier, but at that point the customer will likely be asking you if they can close the sale without the need for you to trigger it, because you revealed the value to them. In doing so, you avoided selling them. Instead you helped them make the decision to buy.

6 REMBERING THE 5 SECRET BUYING VALUES

The concept of the 5 secret buying values makes sense on paper, but putting it to practice always takes a bit of time, primarily because there's a lot to remember as your talking to a customer. You're formulating a strategy, remembering their likes and interests, pain points, facts, etc.

That can make it difficult to remember the key points and trigger points for a customer in relation to the 5 buying values. There's a simply way to remember the 5 buying values however - simply put them in order using your hand.

D Q A P F Practice

Using your off-hand, identify your values in order. Determine what your buying values are for a particular product and assign values to your hand. Set a value to your thumb and fingers in order. Make your thumb the top value; the most important thing.

For example:

Thumb = Design
Index = Quality
Middle = Availability
Ring = Price
Pinky = Functionality

As you engage with customers, you can use the same tactic to remember the values of the customer on the opposite hand.

7 DESTROYING VALUE WITH A SINGLE WORD

Three Letters Away from Poverty

There's a word that has contributed to killing more of your sales than you realize. Not only that, it's been a barrier in other areas of your life. It has contributed to myriad issues in the lives of common people, business men and women, and has single-handedly crashed deals while waiting silently in the wings - a common piece of our vocabulary used every day.

It's used all of the time and we don't see it as a problem. It's among the first few hundred words we learn as a child.

This word can destroy sales, and it's only three letters.

This word acts like an eraser, removing any acknowledgement for the other person and disconnecting what follows from what came before.

"I know what you mean, but ..."

"That might have worked there, but ..."

"Your idea might have some merit, but ..."

In the above sentences, you can see how the word "but" erases the value of the person and their perspective with just a few letters. Imagine what it does to your sales.

To be more persuasive and influential we must remove the word "but" from most conversations. This is important because the word creates division and it causes people to pause. It acutely highlights disagreements while at the same time negating that which came before it, essentially rendering it invalid.

When your goal is to influence a customer toward a sale by highlighting their values, you never want to use the word "but", because it can negate their values. That moves you away from nurturing a relationship with the customer.

Some people have said that but stands for "Behold the Underlying Truth." And when you think about it, it makes sense. When we hear "but" we know that the other person only really wants us to hear what comes next.

The solution to reinforcing the value chain and getting rid of old, unhealthy habits it simple.

A Three Letter Solution

If "but" is a three letter, destructive problem then a solution should be as easy. Replace it with another three letter word.

"And."

"I know what you mean, and ..."

"That might have worked there, and ..."

"Your idea might have some merit, and ..."

There's a notable difference here, and it's easy to see. And is inclusive. It acknowledges and supports what came before it. It reveals possibilities in shades of gray, in the most neutral way possible. It doesn't not stir argument, but instead stirs thought and reveals perspective.

When you're working with a customer through the value chain, it allows them to feel acknowledged, and more open to perspective as you relate things like benefits to their values.

The Underlying Solution

It's a good start to recondition your vocabulary, but you need to go farther. Word choice is a fundamental solution. To be more effective when it comes to sales, you also need an "and" mindset, where you're taking a different approach and being more inclusive, acknowledging and open-minded.

It makes it easier to engage, to actively listen, to understand the customer and to visualize your strategy for leveraging their buying values.

8 BUYER'S REMORSE & THE VALUE CHAIN

We've all experienced buyer's remorse at one point or another. You wanted to treat yourself or reward yourself, so you picked up something you've had your eye on or some kind of electronic toy. After a few days - sometimes the next day - you started wondering if you should have purchased it or not. Where does the feeling come from? Is it because you overspent? Is it guilt for buying something for yourself?

What is Buyer's Remorse?

The term was originally coined to refer to the purchase of a new home, where the owner regretted the commitment after purchasing the property. Now, it's used to reference any number of goods and services. It's normal to consider important decisions carefully, and it is likewise normal to wonder afterward if you've made the right decision.

What's not normal is to worry and regret, letting buyer's remorse get in the way of appreciating and enjoying the item that you purchase.

Do you think people experience buyer's remorse every time they purchase something, or only once in a while? If your friends call you indecisive and you question and berate yourself after making any type of purchase, there could be a larger problem. When you've stepped out of your comfort zone to make an important purchase or choice, it's customary to feel a twinge or two of self-doubt.

You might be asking yourself if you really needed the item. After all, your new stereo might be a great toy, but the older one still works. Maybe you're feeling that you were talked into an unexpected and unbudgeted "extra" with the purchase. You're now holding tickets for first class instead of coach, and you wonder whether it will be worth the additional expense.

It might have been an impulse buy, or you may believe you overpaid and ought to have waited for a sale price. Perhaps you're feeling you were too easily influenced by the wily salesperson who sold you the goods.

That last one has a lot more to do with buyer's remorse than many realize.

Blaming the Salesperson

In many cases, buyer's remorse stems from the guilt that occurs when you break the value chain, or the order of values. In most cases, the salesperson pushes the product and their own values onto the customer, essentially forcing them to focus on values that aren't their own, so they aren't important to the customer. When this type of buyer's remorse occurs, you have one of two results.

1. The customer revisits the purchase in their mind after experiencing the guilt of buyer's remorse. After giving it more thought, they'll justify the purchase by reordering their values and considering the purchase from the point of their priority value followed by the others. Typically if this occurs they wind up selling themselves on it after the fact and no longer feel guilty.

2. The more common scenario is a customer overwhelmed by guilt and remorse. Essentially, they feel as if they cheated themselves. If they can't justify the sale based on their own values, they'll return the product or cancel the service.

In order to avoid buyer's remorse you need stop selling to the customers - instead let them buy from you. Talk to some of the people you know about products they've purchased. Some will say they were sold a new television (or other item), others will say they bought it.

If someone uses the "bought" terminology, they're less likely to feel remorse and they're likely to be happier about the purchase.

People who were sold on something often feel shame, remorse and regret over the purchase and are far less likely to become brand ambassadors for you. In order to get someone to buy from you, where you minimize the sales hype, is to trust in the value chain.

By targeting the buying values, you're helping the customer put emphasis on their own existing values, and you're showing them how the product fits into their values, needs and wants. You're not selling them on the solution; you're simply showing them the path to the solution.

The Cost of Buyer's Remorse

What you have to remember is that a customer doesn't realize they have buying values. All they know is that they purchase a product and at the end of the day they either love it or they feel pushed into it.

If a customer winds up with remorse or guilt, the cost comes back to bite you. Not only do you lose the sales when an item is returned, but they're likely to share their experience with close friends and family - or over social networks. That means the potential for a spread could be from a dozen people to hundreds.

You also lose on the second sales. A product is sold twice, and often as a discount due to repackaging. For a salesperson, that can mean less commission - if any at all - on the resale of a returned item.

What seemed like a routine sale turned into lost revenue, bad PR and unhappy management staring at you.

A problem that is easily fixed by identifying the real values that are important to the customer.

9 SALES PITFALLS THAT BREAK THE VALUE CHAIN

Chapter 8 talked about how the word "but" can wreck your sales and relationship. There are other ways you can sabotage your own sales efforts and destroy any hope of results. While avoiding these should be common sense, it never ceases to amaze me that there are salespeople out there still making these mistakes.

Selling Your Values

This is one of the most common mistakes made by salespeople. With very little research you can come up with the benefits of a product or service as they appeal to you. The offer makes sense, and the salesperson will lead off the sale with what they think is the best value.

This is a good start, but the salesperson will continue to push the other buying values out of order, focusing on features and things that aren't relevant to the customer.

When was the last time you went to a shop and had a salesperson go on about why they like the product? It's annoying, because you don't really care why they like the product. They're asserting their values on you, and imposing their position. This clouds the judgment of the customer, and unfortunately salespeople do this all. the. time.

The only time this works is if you happen to get a customer and a salesperson who share the same value chain. It's rare, but when it happens and the salesperson lands that awesome sale, they think they're golden and they continue with the bad habits.

Unfortunately, the rest of their sales underperform. What's better - having 1 out 5 sales that feel like you've made a new best friend, or 5 out of 5 sales where you feel confident knowing you sold a customer on something they really wanted - because you made them want it.

Not Understanding Customer Needs

Try selling something to someone without talking to them. Walk up to someone on the street and just start talking sales in order to get them to buy a product. If you don't understand their needs, there's no way you'll be successful.

Some salespeople are so concerned about closing sales and hitting a quota that they push for the close without mapping out a strategy to get there, and never really discover what the customer needs.

You won't know if they need it, you don't know what their problem is, you won't know what benefits to highlight or what approach to take and without listening to the customer needs it is impossible to establish the value chain that will help you close.

False Personas

It's extremely common for a salesperson to turn on a smile, become a different person and "lay it on thick" when it comes time to interact with customers. Some people are susceptible to that false charm, but most customers can see through the "used-car salesman" routine.

And it's a great way to sabotage a sale.

The customer will be so focused on you pretending to be something else that they won't be able to apply their full attention to listening to benefits. Even if you have the 5 buying values and value chain development down to the perfect science, you can ruin it by trying to be something you're not.

Always leverage your own personality with confidence. Customers will know when you're being real, and they will greatly appreciate your authenticity.

The Schoolyard Bully

Why any salesperson would every think muscling someone into a sale is a smart idea is beyond me, but there are plenty of people in the business who try to strong arm a customer into a sale. Not physically mind you, by they use imposing stature, fear, lies, exaggeration, over-urgency of missing out, aggressive tones and other tactics that force the hand of the customers.

If it doesn't scare them off, and they actually do purchase, the odds of buyer's remorse are pretty high. There's a clear and obvious line between being a decent human and being a bully in sales. If you've ever been guilty of this tactic, ask yourself: How many sales have you lost because you were too aggressive? How many more do you think can get if you actually try to build honest relationships with customers instead?

Lies

Simply put, lying is bad. Few people in sales start out as bold face liars. What often happens is that they make small exaggerations in order to sell a client on something. In many cases, these little exaggerations aren't often noticed. If the customer does notice after the fact, they don't usually feel cheated because it was small, so you don't typically hear from them.

Unfortunately, the more you exaggerate in order to close sales, the more inflated the exaggerations become until it gets to the point that you're just lying repeatedly in order to appeal to the customer in the best way possible.

If you focus on taking the time to listen, you'll realize that lying isn't necessary, nor is exaggeration. Every customer has triggers based on their values and interests. You just have to find them. Lies are a terrible short cut that can lead to upset customers, lost business, charge backs on commission, consumer complaints, law suits and even charges of fraud.

Lacking Confidence

A salesperson can be shy on confidence for a variety of reasons. Poor sales numbers in a previous quarter, life issues, unfamiliar with a new product, a new market, reprimands and previous or current performance, company layoffs, other work-related problems, etc.

Confidence is an important part of sales. When you're not confident, it shows. A customer can tell during an interaction with sales whether or not the person is comfortable talking through the product or service description and answering their questions.

Confidence comes and goes, but to avoid feeling like you're the one who has to carry the entire sale remember: Don't sell the customer, let them buy. Focus on that primary personal buying value you have and lead off with it to anchor the conversation. Ask that leading question (*Is that what's important to you?*) and let them begin to reveal how to connect with their values.

That engagement not only builds their trust with you, but it will reinforce your confidence as they become more comfortable with you.

Mismatched Corporate Values

Thousands of talented salespeople quit their career and move on each year because of mismatched values. It's the cause of the high turnover rate in telemarketing, and it's why I was forced to rethink the approach to sales with my own teams.

I created scripts and flow charts for sales, but they were based on my values for selling our products. Not theirs, and certainly not in line with the customer. Most companies are like that - with sales approaches based on the buying values of the founder

Every company has values that employees have to live by, and in order to thrive and be successful in sales you need to establish the same communication in a corporate environment that you would with a customer, otherwise you'll pull your hair out trying to do your own thing while corporate demands another route.

Listen, watch and learn from those around you - including the boss - to discern their values. Find where they're in conflict with your own. This gives you new and refreshing insight in the personal buying values of the company. When you understand the environment and the reasoning, the stress to perform verbatim ad infinitum is removed.

Unfortunately, this process only provides insight. There's no single process that can turn every company on to a better way to sell. Your goal would be to remind those you report to that "the boss" is the customer, and in order to get their "yes" then you have to align yourself with their values.

Because their values matter, their concerns matter. After all, they're looking for a solution. If customers really don't care about the product or service, what makes you think they care about corporate values and guidelines for sales?.

10 ESTABLISHING YOUR OWN VALUE CHAIN

Before you can start connecting with customers through active listening and leveraging their value chain, you need to work on your own. As you begin to sell, you're not just making customers feel like they need something or want something enough to bring about a "yes" or achieve compliance.

You're making a mental connection with them by actually understanding their buying values. You understand them because you can relate to them. You recognize what a person needs when Design is their top buying value.

Or you recognize what their concerns and needs are when Functionality is their top buying value.

Most importantly, you recognize your buying values can shift position depending on the product, so if a customer is talking to you about a new 60" flat screen for their media room, and then they also show interest in a surround sound system for the media room, the order of their buying values won't necessarily be the same for those two products.

Salespeople Crush Your Values

Take some time to window shop and see how other people in your industry, as well as other industries, approach you and try to sell you on something. Listen to salespeople, and you'll immediately see that those people tend to press their buying values on you. They don't typically listen to your needs, or wants. They don't understand your value. Most importantly, they don't understand the product and how it can relate to your specific, unique, wants and needs.

One of the tricks to making a strong connection with the customer is owning what you sell.

Now, in some cases it's not practical or even possible to physical own the product or use the service you sell. It may be out of your budget (such as a million dollar service for corporations) it may just not suit your lifestyle. Whatever the reason, you can mentally own the product or use the service without actually engaging in it.

The Mind and Ownership

The mind doesn't really know the difference between visualizing or actually doing something. This is a technique mastered by NASA when they train astronauts for zero gravity and low gravity. You get the body and the mind used to zero gravity by a steep dive in a cargo air where you hang suspended in the air and the astronaut is less likely to vomit in their helmet when they're floating above the earth.

You can condition your mind to own what you sell in the same way.

Why is this important? Because when you're selling something, people will inevitably question you about your personal opinion. If you don't have one, then your response is either going to be "I don't know" or it's going to be a lie.

If you mentally own the product, you can relate to the use and clearly see how the product appeals to different value chains. In addition, you'll be able to speak to a client with the enthusiasm of someone who has real ownership.

You're not only armed with the power to leverage their buyer values, but you've got that spark of passion that can create an instant rapport with the customer.

Make it a regular practice to review as many of your products or services as possible. Go through the process of mentally owning and mentally buying those products.

How would you use it and incorporate it into your lifestyle? How would you feel about using it? What benefits does it provide to you and your family? What would change in your home, personal and professional like if you were to make the purchase?

In order to effectively sell the product, you need to buy it.

As you go through the process of buying, think about the 5 different buying values and how they come up in order of importance while you consider the purchase. What would sell you on functionality, price, design, availability and quality? What would your concerns be?

This can help you create your own personal value chain where each of your products/services are concerned. Once you identify the most important buying value for you, you can effectively lead off with your #1 value position with your clients and speak from a position of ownership and passion.

To effectively do this, you need actually go through the process of buying. Thinking about it while reading this isn't effective, and passively owning your products on a mental whim is as effective as window shopping.

Find the form at: www.the5secretbuyingvalues.com/pvc to run through the exercise on several of your own products and/or services.

Example:

Brian is a sales rep for a luxury car dealership. He wants to improve his sales using the process above and he's never owned one of these vehicles. On a day off, he stops by the dealership and approaches the vehicles as a customer. His first step is visualizing that he wants to buy it, seeing himself using the vehicle and driving it.

Next he begins to handle one of the vehicles. Looking at options from a subjective position - like a customer. Opening doors, looking under the hood, looking at the mpg ratings. As he's reviewing all the options he starts to think about what matters most to him. Is it price? The price is high, but he knows it's worth it for the German engineering. What about the design?

Availability isn't an issue, he knows there's no shortage on production, but it's not a care that's available to everyone. It's a luxury car with a high sticker, so availability is actually low. He could have a car that few others have in the city and really stand out. That lack of availability to others is ability. As he goes through the process of buying the car, he starts to develop his value chain, and it looks like this:

1. Availability
2. Design
3. Price
4. Quality
5. Functionality

After spending time with that particular model, he recognizes the value points in quality (German engineering), the value points in functionality (a lot more options than other models in its class), the value points in availability (exclusivity) and so on.

Brian buys the vehicle mentally, and has revealed to himself how to leverage the value chain on each buying value, no matter the order they're in. More importantly, it revealed to him the most important buying value of that particular product where he is concerned. It's personal to him, and when he engages a customer with it it's going to seem genuine, personal and revealing.

He'll open with his values in a confident way and the customer will really love him for that.

11 WHEN VALUE FAILS

Pushback on Price

I wish I could say that the 5 buying values will give you a perfect close every time, but human factors always lead to some degree of error, and sometimes even 5 yes's will still equate to a no - especially when there is pushback on price.

"Your fees are too high; can you do it for less?"

Every salesperson hears it at one time or another. The easy thing to do is to cut the price and offer a discount, but that always cuts into your profits. In some cases, it can eat up your commission. What's worse is that it sets a precedent for the future and you'll find it next to impossible to get back up to your normal prices on repeat business.

So, what do you do when clients push back on your pricing?

The glib answer is: focus on your value. Trite, but true. If it's worth it to the client, they'll pay for it. But when faced with price push-back, many are at a loss for what to do in the moment, and that can lead to problematic results.

Guidelines to Counter Price Boundaries

Here are five guidelines to follow the next time a prospect says, "Your price is too high."

1. Don't backtrack - I was enjoying a good game of mil-sim paintball some years back and while crawling through some brush with a number of people in my squad, I heard two teammates discussing business. Before I could hush them, one said that the fees for his services were $220 an hour, but he would do it for less if they needed.

That's an example of backtracking before they even got pushback. Why not just cut your prices before offering if you're going to cut prices before they dispute your rates?

Don't fold too soon. Follow the process for connecting via buying values to turn their no into a yes. If the only thing holding them back is price, and you effectively communicate the value, you shouldn't have any problems converting them without having to cut your profits.

2. Confront competitor pricing - Salespeople are often ready to back down on price when someone says they can get XYZ from another provider at a lower price. Instead of acknowledging their price and dropping a discount, just acknowledge that pricing and leave it there.

Communicate directly that you know there are others who charge $X for this product or service but your rates or $X. Then ask the buyer,

"Is there a reason you haven't already rewarded them the business?" Some buyers will share why they'd prefer to work with you, and you can leverage these reasons to maintain your price.

It's true, buyers might walk—that's a risk you take. Many times, however, you'll simply set the foundation for continuing the sales process at your preferred fee level.

3. Don't discuss cost structure - Imagine you're a legal firm with a retainer of $10k per month. Some customers might ask how you come up with the price.

You might then be compelled to pull out a scope sheet and show how some costs are X, the implementation rate is Y, and the monthly service fee is Z, so here's the fee. Heading down this path leads to nickel and diming where a customer may want to drop certain services in order to trim costs.

If you were in the market to buy a car, you don't ask the dealer about the cost of the stereo system, the exhaust or the dash material. The salespeople would laugh at you. In the same vein, you should not lift up the hood simply because a customer asks what your costs are.

4. Don't dismiss the buyer when they push back - In some sales circles I've heard people say that if someone is pushing back on price, then they don't want to do business with them because it's an indication of a high-maintenance or cheap customers.

In my experience, that's rarely the case. Buyers are typically taught to challenge pricing in various ways. Just because they challenge your price or that of your company doesn't mean they're bad people or they have shallow coffers. It also doesn't mean they're challenging your value personally.

Typically, it just means they're trying to figure out how to engage you and your solutions. Some people offer discounts, some don't. They're just asking.

5. Offer payment terms - For some buyers, money is just an issue, and they can't buy because of the payment terms. Sometimes, making an adjustment to payment terms is all a customer needs to move forward and seal the deal.

In the end, customers will pay more for your products and services if they see you offer more value than the alternatives. And as much as you might disdain the thoughts, buyers will continue to pressure price and other consultants will continue discounting to win business. But if you follow these four guidelines when you get price pressure, you'll find yourself winning more deals at your asking price thanks to adherence to the buying values.

12 DISSECTING THE SALES PROCESS

Obtaining Closure

There's always been a drive in sales people to close every deal though, leading to a lot of strategies and refinement of techniques in order to close as many deals as possible. There's no perfect formula, because every customer is different. You have to change in the moment, but the drive remains the same.

That drive to close sales is portrayed in Glengarry Glen Ross, the Oscar-winning 1992 film of the ultimate end all in a Chicago real estate office. "A-B-C." says Blake, the ruthless business man played by Alec Baldwin, who is sent to shake up the sales staff with a contest where the winner gets a Cadillac and the loser gets fired. "Always Be Closing".

Today it's less about closing the deal with less of a focus on money. Yes, money is at the heart of "the close" but the goal is not just selling; it's about booking repeat business and improving the customer relationship, because a repeat customer with a mutually-beneficial, long-term relationship is worth a lot more than a one-off customer.

"The 'close' of the sale is usually described as the point where a prospect or customer agrees to buy. This thinking is very traditional, and should be an obsolete view of the selling process," says Jeff Thull, president and CEO of Prime Resource Group, who has designed and implemented business transformation and professional development programs for companies like Shell Global Solutions, 3M, Microsoft, Siemens, and Citicorp, as well as many fast track, start-up companies. "If you believe the close is the ultimate event, you will no doubt be limited in your success. If you respect your customers and believe they are intelligent individuals with whom you wish to have long-term and mutually beneficial relationships, your goal should be to provide them with products and services that will make them successful".

Closing a Sale: How Great Sales Teams Do It

Closing sales is still the ultimate reason for the process. If you do everything right and don't close the sale, then you were still not successful.

To make things even more difficult, businesses are finding it harder to close sales today than in the past thanks to tough economic times and global competition. Depending on the industry, it could take a salesperson much longer to close because the internet makes competition worldwide.

Given the ability to rapidly research a business and products, and the general state of the economy, buyers are much more cautious about how they invest.

It's important to understand the decisions a customer will be making, and what they need to make, as they move from a point of being outside of your solution, where they don't understand the need for it, to the point where they ultimately decide to acquire it.

The buying values, in addition to other techniques, represent steps in the decision process in any given sequence that are designed to support the succeeding decision.

The Stages of Closing a Sale

There are 5 stages in the basic sale that will move you forward toward the ideal close. They provide a navigable path from identifying potential in the customer, to their decision making process and values that ultimately move you forward.

Stage 1 - Discovery

In this stage, you're working to ensure that the customer matches the profile of the individual or business that you typically find using your products and services. You can't expect or assume that everyone is a customer. Not everyone needs what you're offering.

In order to achieve this, you need to move beyond traditional boundaries of prospecting and start reading the characteristics of the customers. In some situations, background information is enough to lead you in the right direction. In those situations where the first time you meet a customer is the first time you become aware of them, then you continue forward with the next part of the discovery process.

Listening.

Part of the learning process involves listening to your customer. You have to listen very carefully to what the customer or potential customer is saying so that it gives you signals for how to create a win-win and achieve the value close.

It doesn't do any good to smooth talk yourself into a sale today and lose the customer tomorrow.

In order to understand your customer's interest, you need to understand what they want and then fulfill their needs. It's not really relevant to the sales process what you want. What's relevant is what they want. They don't want your product, or your service. They want a solution. You have to listen for the problem in order to know which solution to guide them to, and how to present it to them.

The discover stage will allow you to help your customers understand their inefficiencies and performance gaps, problems, etc. You may be able to help maximize the customer's awareness of their dissatisfaction with their situation, and determine whether that dissatisfaction supports the need for your solution or not.

There are the two major reasons why people do not buy:

1. They don't believe they have the problem or issue that your solution will solve, which includes thinking that the problem isn't big enough to necessitate change.

2. They simply don't believe the solution will work.

Most buyers you deal with fall into the first group, so discovery is critical. Without it, there's no way to know what's impeding their decision. Do they have physical evidence that points to consequences of using the solution? What about in absence of the solution? What is the financial impact in the short term and long term? Is there a notion of unacceptable financial impact that's bothering them? Is the problem even a priority?

You can see where individual questions and concerns relate to the 5 values. By listening, you can discern that someone may be most concerned about cost or quality. This can help you begin building your value chain, and give you a jumping board to lead off with your initial buying value to begin engaging their own values.

The discover stage never really ends. It continues on in the background as you move into other stages, helping you formulate your strategy and establish the buying values of the customer.

Stage 2 - Leading with Confidence

Once you've started to uncover the primary concerns of the customer and their general interest you can begin leading the sale. Leading with confidence is key, because there's no chance of a customer following you and your train of thought when the train is clearly set to derail.

This is where it pays to mentally own your product. If you've gone through the buying process on your own with the product or service you're selling, then you understand what the most important buying value is to you. Lead with this, and reveal that value to the customer and how much it matters to you personally.

Then ask them: *"Is that what's important to you?"*

The engagement continues and the customer will begin to serve you what's really important to them. Even if they reply with a simple "no." you can begin to pull the information out of them. A no is a rare reply, however. People feel compelled to share their needs and wants, and to be social. In most cases, they'll lead off with their most important buying value.

Once you've locked on to that first value you can begin to target the others.

Stage 3 Build the Value Chain

As you engage the customer, continue to gather information as they talk about their concerns in a product or service, the issue they have, other problems they're having, etc. Don't worry about establishing the order of importance. Right now it's about direct engagement with the customer in order to poll information continually.

When you're building the value chain, you're building the relationship. Begin with the foundation and move up from there. It doesn't take long for a customer to tell you what they want or need, and only a little extra encouragement to find out why they're looking at all. As you work through the values and engage the customer, you'll be sharing some of your own values as well. Because you mentally own that product you'll find customers asking you if you own because you seem to be so passionate about it. It's that passion and that mental ownership that drives sales through and moves you toward the final stages.

Stage 4 - Prioritizing the Value Chain

After spending some time with a customer, you've likely got a head full of information you've used to paint a basic image of who they are and what they want. Now you need to think about the priority order of their buying values. Chances are when you asked them what was important to them, they led off with their primary buying value.

The rest of their values are jumbled up by conversation, and based on that conversation you should have a good idea of where they stand with each buying value. If you're not sure, then repeat their concerns back to them and dig a little deeper into each buying value.

Watch for visual and non-verbal cues that can help you recognize the priority of a buying value; raised eyebrows or eye contact when discussing one that is particularly important, or shrugging, a thin-lipped smile or pauses that point to a lack of importance or disinterest in a particular area.

Prioritize the buying values using your right hand, beginning with the primary buying value on the thumb.

Stage 5 - Obtaining the Value Close with 5 Yes's

The value close is simple; once you've ordered their buying values using your hand repeat them back to the customer in order by restating the concern or interest and follow each with "is this correct?"

Values are important to the customer, that's how they base their buying decision. When you're repeating back the values, don't just repeat it like a robot. Mirror them. Talk about those values like you own the product. This creates that amazing connection and the customer will think "Oh my god - this person gets it. They think just like me, my new best friend."

As they connect with you on each buying value and drop a "yes!" they are building that psychological commitment leading up to 5 solid yes statements. At that point, you present the solution that matches the buying values and the needs of the customer

Lastly - do what we do best; ask for the sale and close it.

Closing a Sale - Upselling

For every product or service you sell, there's likely a product or service that can accompany it. Think about what you can do to upsell on every sale, because money makes the world go round - especially if you work on straight commission.

Wall mounts for a television, extra options on a car, rollers and paint pans for paint, belts and accessories with clothing, throw pillows for drapes and more. Tie the products in together and you can effectively increase your bottom line.

This process leaves you wide open for upselling, because you've established credibility and rapport with your customer. They trust you, and they're far more likely to buy into additional products if they think there is value in it.

McDonalds increased their companywide intake by over 20% simply by asking for an upsell with every order. How much would you like to increase your own bottom line by?

If you don't ask, you'll never get a "yes".

The Follow-up

Whether you close the sale or not, always follow up with customers to find out what you can learn from them. The most successful sales people are the ones that have repeat business. The only way to achieve that is to have clients who are happy with what you've provided. It's always a mistake to be so desperate that you have to have this sale today and you don't care what happens tomorrow.

Your customers will have a lot more respect for you when you're truthful about whether your product or service can help solve their problem, and following up proves you are naturally concerned, effectively solidifying your credibility.

If you have formed a solid relationship with your customer, this is your opportunity to use them as a referral engine, effectively driving your sales higher. Lead generation through referrals has been around for a long time, and we have direct sales (MLM and home party industries) to thank for the system.

Allow me to share a story with you;

Back in 1989 I was selling cars, and every time I sold a car I asked for referrals. I would ask satisfied customers for the telephone number of a friend so I could contact them directly. In some cases I asked them to bring a friend in. In almost every instance, they would oblige.

There was always an incentive involved; two movie tickets, a gift basket, cash, a tank of gas, etc. if I was able to close the deal with their friend or associate. I remember a young guy that came in who was strapped for cash, so I made a deal with him.

For every sale I made, he got $100.

That kid brought me 10 sales in the first week, and regular sales for many months!

Remember that getting to "yes" on the 5 secret buying values is only effective if you build relationships and have customers - so work the system in a way that you transform your customers into referral engines. Your customers are one of your best prospecting tools.

13 CONCLUSION - STOP SELLING!

The concept is simple; stop selling and let the customer buy. You're not trying to convince them that they need something. You're trying to reveal their need and connect it with their wants, effectively showing them the most ideal solution and providing them with the benefits of ownership.

In nearly every situation where you effectively prioritize the buying values of a customer and use them to provide a solution, you will achieve the value close. It works because in their mind, it makes sense. You're not trying to sell them on your idea, or your opinion, or your product - you're simply saying

"From talking with you, you said 'A, B, C, D and E' are your primary concerns. I have an ideal solution and this is how it addresses those concerns".

As you move through the 5 buying values with a customer, it's like slowly sliding the right key into a lock. The tumblers fall into place one by one until eventually, you can turn the key and the doorway opens.

That door leads into the secret place in the mind of a customer where their decisions are made. If you can get inside that room, it's easy to draw them out and close the sale.

Now - use this knowledge to change your own game. I challenge you to review this content at least 3 times and commit the process to memory.

Go and own your products, complete the worksheet then put the process to action. You'll see a noticeable difference in how your customers respond - and in your profit!

After you've been using this sales approach, I want to hear from you. Email me and connect with me in social media. Let me know about your results and success.

ABOUT AUTHOR

"Whether we're talking about selling for $1 or $1 million, it's all the same to me. It's a sale!"

While Matthew currently resides in Norway, he is a Kiwi by nature with roots deep in New Zealand. He has been in business his entire life, guided by his mother (who he claims was by far the best sales person in the world.)

A self-proclaimed veteran serial entrepreneur of 25 years, Matthew has a spirit for sales and success, striving to sell in the footprints of his mother. Matthew was born with a fiery spirit, the kind that drives people to one of two places: Utopian Success or Complete Madness. With the launch, growth and sale of several businesses, including ROCKA Furniture of Norway, there's proof that success is his driving factor.

Matthew spent years training sales staff and refining his sales process over numerous industries such as car parts, vehicles, telephone sales, retail, B2B, B2C, network marketing and more. He has trained thousands of network marketers and has spoken to countless companies, retail chains, banks and automobile dealerships.

Matthew is a best-selling author, with contributions in a wide range of books relating to health & wellness, business strategy, professional branding and online marketing along with the book Counter-Attack: Business Strategies for Explosive Growth in the New Economy which was co-authored with Brian Tracey. Matthew's career and many endeavors, including published works, have taught him that nothing can be achieved by watching, but everything can be achieved by doing.

*

'Listen to the customer's mind, not their words"

Matthew E. Alleyne

*

ADDITIONAL INFO AND RESOURCE

For additional forms and exercise worksheets, register and login at www.The5SecretBuyingValues.com

From there you can also follow my blog for regular sales tips as well as watch online sales courses to refine your techniques and get that close.

Live seminars, webinars and educational products will be available via special offers.

For affiliate information, where you can earn money selling this book or any of our products, you can visit and enroll in the affiliate program at:

www.The5SecretBuyingValues.com/affiliate-program or
www.T5SBV.com/affiliate-program

Contacting Matthew for Coaching and Consultation

I travel the world teaching in a variety of venues, corporate environments and in small business/sales workshops. With the range provided, I can talk one on one for coaching purposes or address large audiences.

I also offer full-service online marketing solutions through MyBrandButler.com If you're interested in booking me for a speaking engagement regards sales, branding or marketing, or your company is interested in marketing services you can contact me with the information below.

The services we provide have encourage growth in a variety of industries including direct sales and networking marketing. If you have a desire to grow, and you feel that change is needed in order to obtain your goals, don't hesitate to contact me.

To Your Sales Success,

Matthew E. Alleyne

matthew@mybrandbutler.com
Phone: +1 855 866 8489
www.The5SecretBuyingValues.com
www.MyBrandButler.com
Facebook: www.facebook.com/thetootguy
Facebook Page: www.facebook.com/the5secretbuyingvalues
Twitter: www.twitter.com/t5sbv
Twitter: www.twitter.com/thetootguy

NOTES

NOTES

READ 1 – 2 – 3 TIMES

I challenge you to review this content at least 3 times and commit the process to memory.

Matthew E. Alleyne

www.ingramcontent.com/pod-product-compliance
Lightning Source LLC
LaVergne TN
LVHW050937080826
845145LV00004B/1306

* 9 7 8 8 2 9 9 8 8 9 8 0 3 *